A GILDED LAPSE OF TIME

A GILDED
LAPSE OF TIME

GJERTRUD

SCHNACKENBERG

Farrar Straus Giroux / New York

Library of Congress Cataloging-in-Publication Data
Schnackenberg, Gjertrud.
A gilded lapse of time / Gjertrud Schnackenberg.—1st ed.
p.   cm.
I. Title.
PS3569.C5178G5   1992
811'.54—dc20   92-13462CIP

Grateful acknowledgment is made to The Yale Review, where "Angels Griev-
ing over the Dead Christ" and "Tiberius Learns of the Resurrection" first ap-
peared, and to The New Yorker, where the following poems first appeared:
Sections 1, 2, 3 and 20 of "A Gilded Lapse of Time"; sections 5 and 6 of "A
Monument in Utopia"; and "The Resurrection."

For their generous support during the time this book was written,
the author would like to thank the Guggenheim Foundation,
the National Endowment for the Arts, the Amy Lowell Traveling Scholarship,
and especially The American Academy in Rome.

TO MY HUSBAND, ROBERT

CONTENTS

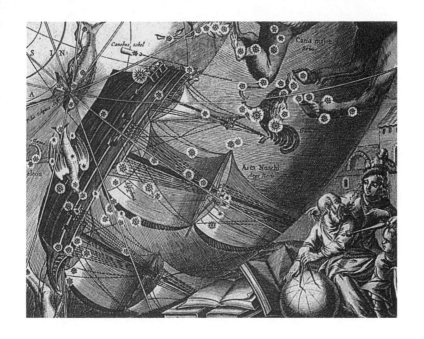

PART ONE

A GILDED LAPSE

OF TIME

A GILDED LAPSE OF TIME

(Ravenna)

1. The Mausoleum of Galla Placidia

When love was driven back upon itself,
When a lapse, where my life should have been,
Opened like a breach in the wall, and I stood
At a standstill before the gate built with mud,
I thought my name was spoken and I couldn't reply—
Even knowing that when you hear your name
It's a soul on the other side who is grieving
For you, though you're never told why.

Among the hallowed statues of dead stalks
I stood, where the rosebush was abandoned by
The pruning shears, among the stumps of brambles
Near the muddy door to the next life.
There was a rubbish mound at the ancient gate
And a broken branch the gardeners had tossed
Toward the leaf pile, scattering its gold dust
Before the doorway carved, as if into a hillside,
Into a frozen room raised in the desolate
Outskirts of Byzantium, where now an industrial zone
Pressed toward the porch of an ancient church
Built in the fulfillment of a vow,
Where the Byzantines would lay aside
Their musical instruments in order to enter
The sanctuary unaccompanied; I stood

Uncertain at the threshold of a pile
Of enigmatic, rose-colored brick, a tomb
A barbarian empress built for herself
That conceals within its inauspicious,

Shattered-looking vault the whirl of gold,
The inflooding realm we may only touch
For one instant with a total leap of the heart—
Like the work of the bees who laid aside
Their holy, inner craft because the Lord
Whistled for them, and they fled
To Him, but long ago, leaving behind
These unfinished combs from biblical antiquity
We are forbidden to touch, still deep
In the wood's heart, still dripping on the ground.

Then a tour guide beckoned me in,
And lifted her flashlight beam to the low vault
Of the Second Rome, brushing the white,
Fifth-century, barbarian stars with gilt,
And I could hear the snowflakes gathering overhead
In the treasure vaults of snow from another age,
In vaults where the snowflake is begotten,
Where angels crowded toward us, inquisitive,
In Paradise, where they'd long ago forgotten
That God repented after He made man,

Where the doves had built their summer palaces
With green grass plucked from underneath
The bare feet of the blessed, and gold glass glowed
As if embers from the imperial furnaces
Had breathed behind the walls, were breathing
From the sphere where love is kindled,
Even if that sphere was broken long before
Our births—but when I pressed
My palm against the uneven, glittering stones,
To the touch they were winter-desolate.

Then objects in heaven began to throb.
Though overlaid with your planets, Dante,
Your stack of nine heavens, your God the Father
Above the hollow spheres, and the eight hundred stars
Drawn into the plaster by the Pictor Imaginarius
That still throb in a Byzantine horoscope
No one will ever bother to cast again—

Still, the hammered gold in rooms all through
Byzantium conceals the pictureless underworlds
Of mortar slathered by the workmen's trowels,
And the vaults' dead spaces are held up
By supporting empty earthenware jars
Still intact, still holding up the stars
In the dome-shaped fog of gold that stands
As motionless as the huge globe you walked
From end to end, beginning here below—
Not like those vessels God had wanted to use
In creating the world but which broke in His hands.

3

Dante, in Paradise, as you climbed,
Earth was only a word, earth was only the place
Where you had died, where you had hidden
The *Paradiso*'s ending behind a wall
And it began to molder after you died.
You'd long ago left behind the cliffs of hell,
The immaterial mountain, the sphere of the moon,
But the sight of His face, of the book of love unbound
And scattering its leaves, you hid away
In a blank, unmarked place on the wall beside
Your deathbed, where your descendants could scrape
With a knife or a broken branch, not daring
To say aloud what they were looking for—
The ending, pointed out in a dream.

I have visited every fountain in the guidebook,
And loitered at the crumbling rims
Of baptistry fonts whose quarter-inch
Of water lies gilded beneath
The ceiling mosaic's tremorous, rhythmic hymns,
Where God is a word written into the ceiling
Under planets shining even by day—

And outdoors in the city traffic,
I've crossed and recrossed these city squares
As if I were pacing them off, as if
I had dropped everything to come and look,
As if there were nothing to do but thumb
The index for the names of goddesses
Who cried at these sites and springs arose
Beneath their feet, so that, ever since,
Throughout the mosaics across Ravenna's ceilings
A streak of blue perpetually flows,
An upwelling crux of radiance in the grasses
That draws animals in search of healing,

Stags whose horns flash as they bend to drink,
Peacocks taking refuge at the springs,
Lambs with drops of water on their muzzles,
Doves mesmerized at the edge of a birdbath
Where a parched leaf whirls at the brilliant cliff
The water makes along its edge before it falls
Among holes like dried-up waterfalls
That wore channels through the bricks, breaking open

Upon ever deeper, ever hastier depictions,
Pictures sealed within pictures, of water boiling
Behind the bricks before it swamped the room
With a glistening mirage, dry to the touch

Though once these streets were canals, once inhabitants
Complained in the civic registers of terrible
Smells stirred up by the bargemen's poles,
Once the waters rose so high the citizens
Were drowned in their houses, in floods whose chronicles
Lay open in my room last night, depicted
On parched paper as a succession of tides
Boiling through the dark ages—a deluge
Marked by a flood tablet on a street corner,

Where the fountains have lain choked for centuries
As if Justinian, with a reckless word,
Had expelled the water from the city, so that
The fountains also of the deep and the windows
Of heaven were stopped, and the rain from heaven
Was restrained—and he heard in his far-off rooms
On the other side of Asia Minor
Ravenna's blackbirds crying and crying for rain,
Beating at the eaves for a drop of water,
His palace ceilings haunted by their cries for mercy,
And in remorse had ordered his engineers
To inscribe a dome the size of Calvary
With Latin letters spelled in gold rain,
Hinting at other, unmarked deluges reeling

Past the rooflines in churches across the city
Where angels lift the drapes aside to show
Yet another fountain pictured in the ceiling.

5. San Vitale

Now in a gilded apse the celestial globe
Has rolled to the end of an invisible rope
And come to rest on a cliff in a blue-green garden.
I look up, as if nothing had killed my hope,
At a blue sphere, buoyant in the sixth-century tides
Still surging and dying away through San Vitale,
Where a spring has glinted in the numinous
Fresh-cut grass for more than a millennium
And never has evaporated or flooded over,
Though it is cracked in a million places, a dried
Streambed the Messiah has walked in search of water.
He leans back, white-faced, to say *I thirst*
Among rosebushes He threw His robe across
In exhaustion and thereby carelessly blessed—

Bright traces of those ancient floods
Shine above the vanished altar, fed by the old motif
Of four rivers whose names I am unsure of,
Four heavenly rivers pouring overhead
From the next world, backward into this,
But they shiver and draw back, suspended above our heads,
Hanging, in the mosaics, like icicles
Unable to pour their healing waters over us,

Though glinting through a hole at my feet
There is a flood remnant, reflected in the apse,
As if the Samaritan woman's water jar
Had been hurled against the wall, and still was dripping
Into the long-lost relics' burial place;

Or it may be only a freshly washed floor
Whose little lakes are dashed from a metal pail
And swept around by the custodian's mop—
I cannot tell. But they say the ice-cold well
Of martyrdom brims into the present here,
They say this is the hollow-hidden font
Where fragments of lost names illegibly
Shiver behind an ancient grille.

There the human being is the vision all my life
I was tutored in, there the *imago Dei* wavers
Above the flooded, inaccessible crypt,
A radiant blur, reflected, elusive among
Supporting columns knee-deep in cold water
Routinely drained by an invisible pump—
We are water that is spilled on the ground
Where Jesus ripples outward, his hand outstretched;
His palm lies open, lifted and upheld
On the jet of an invisible fountain
Cohering from an undulating hush,
Though hints of other, higher, atrocious waters
Tower in the apse's gilt peripheries,
Where a thousand years may intervene between
One glimpse and another, between the coming to
Of the water-resurrected image and what
My heart still struggles with, and still cannot
Surrender up to you,

Messiah, banished to an apse so crushed beneath
A Visigoth's pillaging axe, you felt the blow,
So crushed even the Empress could take fright—
She whose deeds panicked the chronicler—
Even she could dash the stolen suffering cup
At the fountain, and raise her cupped
Palms to catch the cascading hexameter-streams
Of Byzantine hymns, engulfed by the stone sea,
Praying with hidden face, standing apart:

Messiah, do not withdraw your hand from me.
Messiah, looking back where we have gathered
On the stone floor—looking through crazed gold,
As if you'd raised yourself to gaze at us,
Astonished, through a broken window's heart.

Far below I rest my hand against the stones
The workmen laid in 547, when they believed
A hollow sphere encompassed us, when they thought
That there must exist spheres, made
Of the fifth essence, situated in the depth
Of the universe, and moving there,
Some higher up, some arranged below them,
Some larger, some smaller, some hollow,
And some massive within the hollow ones,
To which the planets are fastened,
Each axis fixed on the surface of the one
Surrounding it, and seven planets wheeling
Under God's omnipresent shadow, where now

At the scaffolding before the Sacrifice of Isaac
The aproned workers of a restoration team
Lean from their wooden balcony, urging me
To climb a ladder through the scaffolding
To join those angels seated in the cold church
At a feast table beneath a leafy oak,
Three angels who turn their eyes away
Lest they come face to face with God breaking a law
In the white gaps the sacred text still haunts,
Lest they witness Abraham's unrecorded response,
Lest they see his knife raised for the death stroke—
I hear the world brake on its axis
And come to a halt at the foot of the wall
I rest my hand on; I hear a rope wobble, lashing
The globe back and forth in a scourge of gold snow

That parts on the sight of other ceilings,
Other chains, other heights from which
Other worlds hang, and a book creaks open
In the stars above Isaac's head:
Oh, slam this book shut! God, do not show us!
But the angels do not look, scrupulous in
Honoring the law in Paradise that no one may
Observe the suffering of humans here below—
Not even in that ancient time when God
Reached down to interrupt the sacrifice,
As if He hadn't meant to hurt us so—
We'd not yet driven Him into the high gilt corner
Of a tesserae-shattered wall where a workman
Touches a flake of gold leaf in the hem
Of His threadbare gown with a tweezers woefully small.

8

I sit on the scaffolding near where God
Is deafened, haggard on His mercy seat,
The stars around Him covered with black cloths
Lest they hold His dying day in awe,
The lower section of His throne hidden partially
With scaffolding and drapes, as if He had wrapped up
The black, jagged star that overhung Byzantium,
Wound it up in a cloth and stowed it beneath His throne.
Then *look no more upon't!* Then *pluck it off!*
Our fault has aged you, driven you off, our fault
Has pressed you into this inaccessible vault
Where you are the Lord of a stone floor
That boiled up so long ago you can't recall,
Where you've forgotten that you made the world
To boil at its heart with boiling stone—

Overhead, the scribe Isaiah holds a scroll,
And though the mortifying coal, the supernatural ember,
Had scorched his lips—
Isaiah gazes down from a gold-leafed tower
At those of us stranded in the aftermath,
He gazes down from the heights of his poetry,
He gazes down as if his poetry had not driven
Jesus along the muddy path.

9

Lord, we cannot discern
The guilt of our callings—
Let me turn away, at fault, and overawed;
Let me say, *You are still my Lord and my God,*
Let me say I am unable to ascertain
The guilt of poetry, and leave a prayer scribbled
In the gold room where the written word
Presses us back—
You are the God
Of a word we have not learned,
And the *verbum visibilum* really does
Flicker in the gilt fog of the apse
Where it once burned.

Now in alabaster-mullioned galleries
The mosaics are a bank of gold snow
Deposited by a half a million afternoons,
A twinkling reef of crud,
A cliff of lowering cold that pushes
Toward the ladder's edge, where
One world passes into the next as the earth
Slowly revolves away from the sinking apse
Beyond the scaffold ledge,
Where God's hand hangs empty above
The depiction of frightful laws
As if He tried to plunge
His hand into a bank of gold snow
Covered with grime,
To grasp at least a handful

Of Creation, to remember it by,
But what He touches thaws,
And starts to trickle through itself,
Then streams off through His hand,
Downward, through the gilded lapse of time.

10. At Dante's Tomb

In the cypress zone behind your tomb,
Between two worlds, there was a gash
Where *the creation was subjected*
To futility, like a hole
Where a cross was planted once,
Like a dead fountain, dismantled
And carted off in the spoil wagons
Of Charlemagne,
Like a lost foundation dug up by a dog,
Like a hole dug out by rain.

Now, in the grass, what's left
Is the buried pavement
Long since broken up,
Numbered, and hauled off
To a museum crypt,
And the foundations of the bell tower,

From the time when
The grime-scrubbed
Throne of Maximian
Was merely an empty ivory chair,
Merely a throne abandoned in a grassy field
With a great crack running across the back,
A gash inflicted
In a crisis so severe
In the wake of the invasions they'd lost track
Of calendars, planetary
Epicycles, holy years,

Though marauders spared
The purple cushion without price,
Fashioned in Ravenna's silk shops,
That loomed on the otherwise empty throne
Of the Redeemer—
Now the narrow puddles
In the thorn brake are radiant shrouds
Left lying in the grass overnight,
Shining in the garden
As if Ravenna's
Citizens were resurrected here.

With drenched stockings,
Ankle-deep in wet grass,
I lower my foot to fathom
A depression in the grass,
Like a biblical cleft
In the rock, in an oceanside town
From which even the ocean has withdrawn
Beyond a marsh
Whose fever plague swept
You off, though now the sea is four miles away—
Where the Greek Exarchs built
Their guardhouses and privies, their furnaces
For glassworks, their sewer drains
And smokestacks, their chapels evanesced

In a whirl of rain
That hurls itself from that age to my feet,

Among the empty sarcophagi
Strewn around
The medieval grounds, where the Judgment
Tore off the humblest stone lids
But left undisturbed the rich men's
Marble graves, where the resurrection
Is only for marble caterpillars
Sculpted in their shrouds,

Though nearly induced,
Nearly transmogrified,
Nearly pulsing like butterflies
Shaken from a sack
Into the freezing church,
Like rhymes you shook into blizzards
Still circling back
Six hundred years above Ravenna
And never alighting
Among the glittering floors and marble lakes
Of monuments that sheltered you.
Rain slants, crashing into puddles
Where, among the lost graves of the poor,
I lean over, looking into
The mirrored, northern edge

Of the Western Roman Empire grown over
With stiff grass,
Where the long-vanished basilicas
From here to Classe

Still waver like images
Rendered in shrouds,
Petriana, San Severo, and the one so long-lost
Its name is absent even from
The ancient documents,

Vanished apses,
Buoyant above the water table,
Where the bloody story still
Is recounted overhead
In blurry detail,
Where the executioner stands
Like a rose sprung up at the foot of the cross
Wearing a mask of bees
In the circle of those
Who stood together on the Mount of Paradise,
And Jesus wears on His head
The excruciating radiance.

But when I bend down
To peer through the overgrown grass,
Speeding toward me suddenly rivers of butterflies
Undulate into my eyes
So that I quickly straighten up—
There is only a road laid through a gray cloud
To a marsh, a difficult approach
To a sagging mound of bricks, and a few bushes
I can't name, scraggling in a dripping lane,
And grass running toward the docks

Of the imperial fleet,
Silted over, or floated off across the Adriatic;

I lower my foot
As if a holy stream were running past,
As if the puddle held a rain-bright cross,
Then reach down to touch
This fragment of the northern hemisphere,
To riffle and disturb
An empty place the rain is rending,
A hole spreading above the world,
A drift of dark reflected—

Not the river like a strip of light
Into which you plunged your face, in Paradise,
Letting it cascade from your lashes,
Only a raindrop
On my lashes into which
I look in time to see
A black star drawing near
Plunge past my peripheral sight,
And disappear.

11. At Dante's Tomb

In English *world* is an isolated sound,
With an unmistakable, audible, inward whirl,
Tilted on a hum that rhymes with itself,
Revolving when we speak it, then ceasing to spin.
We may founder before it, stranded before the page
Where we gaze at it from above,
Though if we say *worldworldworldworldworld*
We can feel it beginning to spin around
Its axis, then brake to a halt
When we turn our attention away. You believed
We intuit the sound of the spheres, Dante,
When God touches our ears. *Ephphatha. Be thou opened.*

For you the earth was motionless, silent,
Suspended, except that it gaped with hell,
With a distant reverberation underfoot,
A din you heard rising from the world's
Shattered insides where those without hope
Rave and beat on the ground.

But stranded on the cliff's edge
Of your death mask, and older than you were
That morning when you began to take the way down
Into hidden, gigantic dimensions,
Over the sides of diminishing terraces
I can't bring myself to peer from—
Here on earth, in the room above
The temple they built on your tomb,
I circle around

And reappear, an apparition in midair
In the glass case where your death mask shows
The likeness of a man who, closing his eyes,
Holds still in order to discern
A very faint sound.

Lying among gifts from continents you didn't see
Even from heaven, and a sack of laurel leaves
D'Annunzio hefted here in homage
To the original withered remnants of a crown
They found among your bones, like a lost branch

Fallen from that ancient gunnysack of thorns
Cain trundles on his back across the moon,
But someone else's moon, not ours, one of
Those moons which circles . . . Jupiter . . . Neptune . . .

Your mask lies, petrified into a bronze model
Of lunar cliffs at whose base you were stranded
And could ascend only by having a dream of ascent;

This mask, a speechless record of the moment that,
When shining forcefully upon you God
Beat back the weakness of your gaze, you
Were blinded by the radiance of love, and you left behind

This mask—as if you'd groped your way back here
Across a barrier of thorns, to find
A makeshift throne of rock, and took your seat
In a city of empty thrones and headless crowns,

Still wearing the lopsided, shattered wreath
Ravenna crowned you with after your death,
When you were lifted through Ravenna's streets—
The laurel crown refused, withheld, forgone,

Now scattered on a wooden museum shelf
Before your blinded gaze, you who were crowned—
Before you crossed the threshold, where you saw
The stars grow larger, brighter than they ever looked
From Florence or Ravenna—lord of yourself.

14

But these remnants from the tree of poetry
Could be the leaves you gathered up
After that accident in the second wood,
After that wound, inflicted inadvertently,
That welling in the bowl of an injury
You could not stanch or bind with a rag,
That babbling injury at the root of speech
From a speechless depth you'd torn into that soul:
Why do you break me? Why do you tear me?
Something whose suffering you understood
But thought too sacred to be said aloud.
And as for me, once I had seen that seeping
At the root of that outcry, I kept to myself,
Afraid that if I spoke, my tongue would
Touch those mutilated words, I was afraid
That if I spoke I would taste blood: Don't tear
The leaves off the tree of nonexistence,
Don't pull them bleeding and crying from the branch!
Leave the unconceived alone, unborn!
Leave them hidden above this smear of blood!
If you would love them, do this much for them,
To let them be. Or that is what I heard
When I thought poetry was love, and I had
Sickened of poetry.

I would lay open before my God
That nine and twentieth year of mine age.
I would lay open those years that I could not
Speak. Years I could only thumb the page
Into featureless velvet, unraveling the bleary gilt
Where the kingdom had glinted but guttered out,
Where I copied out your verses by hand
In a foreign language, and as I wrote I could see
Those rhymes throb down the length of the page
And that sound—a glimpse of that sound,
After which everything I had scribbled
In my own hand came to a weightless bundle,
But what foundered beyond the page was more
Than I could lift, more than could be enshadowed
Even in a private script in the margins—

Though here on earth letters
Do not cast shadows, as you did,
Dumbfounding the dead,
Still, lying across
That white realm of silence,
Such pictures are formed
I would lower a ruler into hell
To measure its depth,

But when I run my palm over the page
Those hovering magnitudes evaporate,
Leaving flat paper, without depth;
My fingertips can feel nothing there,
Or else the letters
Have joined their shadows,
And cleave to them,
Spelling out in the white silence
A black, intangible script,
A catechism of existence without objects,
Though I read to myself, moving my lips—

As if I could take my mind off
That outpouring from the branches,
Where you tore the letters
From silence, as if to hurt that soul,
As if purposely to draw
A scent of bloodspill,
Where my pencil
Unwittingly had inscribed a black star

In the margin, beside the verse that pours
Its weeping question out to you—then
I turned away from that sudden cry
In the black-leaved void,
Leaving you there, speechless in the wood;
I turned away
To scramble out of those deepening
Cliffs that hang at our feet;
I grasped at a branch,
And wounded it, tearing it
To pull myself up—

Though if I could have clenched
That crud of leaves in my fist,
Until a sludge of gold seeped to the surface,
I would have pressed the leaves
In reverence to my lips.

Then the evening bell struck thirteen in your honor
And I returned to the sound of my own lips.
But when the museum guard hauled shut at my heel
The heavy, consecutive doors they've set
Into your tomb, hauling with all his weight
As if he were the seraph responsible
For the operation of the great wheels, for
The turning of the slowest of the spheres—
I heard a deeper set of doors slam shut,

A sound reverberating outside the walls of poetry,
As if the doors of the kingdom had closed behind me
With that sound you could not transcribe
After you'd crossed the threshold of the dead
And entered a gate from which you promised
Never to look back, no matter what,

As the doors slammed shut,
And you let your thoughts revolve
Around the bliss of leaving your life behind,
Of clinging in your ascent, and looking up,
Forgetting earth with every step you took—

Dante, in Paradise, as you climbed,
From the starry paths you must have seen
The mansions that stood uninhabited

In empty Florence, grass pushing through the floors,
The stairway to your father's house become
A stairway up to other people's doors

In city squares with unfamiliar names;
You must have seen the city's marble squares
Crowded with strangers and their descendants,

Roads choked with future people streaming away,
Their backs to you, and if they turned around,
You would not know them; you must have seen

Their lives were simply other people's wars—
And, farther back, you must have seen yourself
Driven back upon a sequence of nativities

In stony hill towns, an enemy of Florence,
Traveling west to east, through Golgothas
In blizzards of gold, on peeling walls,

In shadowy plaster, in smoky oils
Shadowing forth, the letter X formed
Out of angels revolving above all those

Upturned faces in driving rain joined by your own.
But in fact you often loitered there alone,
Peering up, not into the heavens as you thought,

But into the low, smoke-blackened ceilings;
In fact, you often paced, not the terraces
Of Purgatory, but only your borrowed study,

Looking down, not from Paradise, but from
The second story, into a dreary province
Lit from the north and stretching through a marsh

Among Roman sarcophagi, in a backwater
Formerly a capital, barren of ideas;
You stood stock-still, not in the shadowless

Grass with angels, but in the icy garden lanes
Of the Count who sheltered you, still postulating
The existence of another heaven outside

The heaven of the stars, still intuiting
The glint of the primum mobile flashing east
To west with that beautiful shimmering, that trepidation,

Whose movement is swift beyond all comprehension,
Without which the planet Saturn would be hidden
From every place on earth for fifteen years,

The planet Jupiter for six, the planet Mars
For nearly a year . . . *She had lived in this world*
For the length of time in which the heaven of

The fixed stars had circled one twelfth of a degree
Towards the East . . .
But even then your poem began to unwind

Its road before your feet, along which you hurried
Through the marsh-plain back to Florence,
The road where you anxiously hailed and overtook

Events, conversations, persons long dead,
Other exiles of other people's cities,
As at your back, along the Adriatic coast,

The sunset's whirling towers would collapse
And buckle through the gates they tore
Into themselves, melting sideways into the sea,

Floating there in swirls of scarlet-lilac,
Then darken and go under silently,
And then: *the luminous sphere of Mars,*

As if a city-state would turn its powers
Of banishment against itself so easily,
And melt away, so you could see the stars.

But as for me, standing
Among blank rocks,
After that door was shut, I turned
And hurried away. After that sound,
I hurried along the road
Toward my hotel, beneath the heavenly city
Visible when one emerges into the night,
Past the Law Giver's
Holy domes, where He promulgates
The laws of bliss whereby we are meant
To turn our backs on the pain
Of the condemned when we're forgiven;

I hurried past
The utopian arcades of the entrance
To the Basilica Metropolitana,
The disbanded workshops
For the manufacture of gold glass,
Past numberless empty tombs
And acres of church floors
Still strewn with gold-glass cubes
Like splinters of the spheres
Lying crushed beneath our feet,
Past street signs pointing
To Theodoric's dome,
A cracked sphere
Fallen from the sixth century
Into a ring of desolate suburbs,
Perpetually shrouded in its Ostrogothic dusk;

I hurried beneath the stars
To my hotel,
To the reading lamp's
Blindness-inducing aureole,
The intangible, brilliant sphere
Through which I could pass my hand,
Watching it float above
Your Purgatory, your dream weightless as
You walk the world from end to end,
Then touch the starry paths.

But when I turned out the lamp,
And stood a moment on the cold tiles in my room
As if underneath that roof from the dark ages,
Where I had tried to shake off
The old chill, though night,
In a rented room, is a kingdom too—
Then I turned to my God;
I looked outside;
Beyond the window ledge of my room,
Above the roofs of the city,
The curving height

Where the night creation glittered—
I looked, to try to fix it in my sight,
I raised my eyes to the high wheels,
I tried to turn with you to see
That point at which the fixed stars
Twinkle in translations,

Where one motion and another cross,
Where east and west mingle
With unfamiliar orbits and constellations
Before which we could grow
Forgetful, as if our lives and deeds
No longer mattered—were it not that
We still hear that weeping there below.

20

Then Gabriel sent down a dream that I stood
Holding a broken-off branch in the wood's heart,
And turning around, I saw the gate built with mud

From the other side, and flights of stairs above my head—
I had passed through it, and the branch I found myself
Holding shrank in my arms and withered away.

Fastened above the gate, a broken honeycomb
Like the concave interior of a death mask
Knocked from an ancestral frieze

Gaped: I had struck it—I had meant only
To open your book, to study poetry's empty beauty,
Not to rest my hand on two featureless tablets of wax

Fashioned with honeycombs in the age of kings,
The combs a poet touches to his lips,
Seeking to cross the threshold, to signify

A sacred conversation. I had broken
The reliquary of the bee, where she had sifted
Her yellow powder through melismatic generations,

Worlds, numberless lifetimes, seeking to finish
Her combs, to mix a flower-dust paste and fix
One drop to the blank mask of her catacomb,

To the brink of a miniature chasm—we are meant
To open a hive with reverence, but instead
I had broken the hive apart with a branch, and worse,

I had left the honeycomb dripping on the ground
In the wood's heart, a profanity
Of waste, and the bees whirled into my ears

Their endless sequences, their burning rhymes
I groped among for what I meant to say.
Angels were there, and one of them turned

And struck me when I spoke, and I lifted my hand
And touched blood on my mouth, and then I saw
They were holding an impression from your face—

Or rather a heavy honeycomb, and your words
Were a stream of bees floating toward me in sunlight.
When I opened your book I thought you spoke,

Or else it was Gabriel lifting to my lips
A tablespoon of golden, boiling smoke
So wounding to my mouth I turned my back

On the source of poetry, and then I woke.

PART TWO

CRUX OF

RADIANCE

ANNUNCIATION

I

Rumors lash the angel's robes
Into transitory statues
Madly overturned,
But they disappear without breaking.

The grasshopper standing near the wall
Like a remnant of the plague
Has turned her face away,
Quadrupled in shadow on the bricks,
Undisturbed by what takes place in heaven,
She fiddles her psalm of grief
Again and again, seventy times seven,
Letting her composition unfurl
Waves of black oxygen.

And the paper wasp has left off
Weaving a death mask
For Augustus, in a secret place,
And arrived to touch the wall uneasily,
Seeking a way to blindly touch
The angel's face,
To prepare for a future measuring.

Outside, in a narrow court of stone,
Where a broom leans against a heap
Of debris, where Rome is piled up on Rome,
King Herod is a beggar in the lane,
And the handful of gravel he
Offers with an averted face,
In his outstretched palm,
Was once Jerusalem—

The gravel of ritual objects,
Temple remnants, broken tablets, a handful
Of pulsing coals whose catacombs
Are airy mazes where human cries
Were torn out by the roots,
Torn word by word,
Like gold nuggets from the Roman mines,
But silent now, twinkling,
As if nothing had occurred.

3

Herod, trying to build
A crooked door
Out of King David's wrecked harp
Looted from the Temple,
Sets the harp frame upright,
Then turns to gesture others in,
But discovers himself alone
In the little Jewish village.
And the harp is an opening
Through which angels have swarmed
And disappeared from the roads;
The harp is an opening like the mouth
Of King David, upon which a speechless
Psalm is formed.

Where is everyone?
They lie captured
In the holds of ships,
They are stuffed in a narrow hole,
They are slaves in an alien marketplace,
And horses drag them by the hair.
They are sold off to the mines.
The last person is slain
In the bath and there is
No one left to put to the test.

There was a battle
No one bothered to record
Since there were troubles enough.
An upheaval on such a scale that
Afterwards, through the temple porches
Strange planets from a glittery hoard
Were swimming past.
There were heavy rains
Through which the people
Struggled north.

Leaning against the wall,
An axe handle Joseph made
For an axe that Azrael seized
From Joseph's hands
And wielded so recently
The vine blossoms still gasp
Along the blade.

5

When Azrael entered the road,
All the brooms withdrew
From the stoops.
All the doors
Slammed shut in the streets.
One by one the grinders
Ceased to grind the grain.
When Azrael passed by a house,
All the knives were reground,
The pottery broken and quickly swept away—
In Azrael's path,
Shattered plates in a mound.
Now, if a loom's shuttle was found
To be carved out of wood that had grown
From the grove of ground
Over which the angel had passed,
The shuttle would be destroyed.

But Azrael halts, and says to the air:
I too must drink from a broken cup.
I too must sit at the choked fountain.
I too have a fragment of the void
Lodged in my brain.
He fingers broken threads that hang
Like relics of the silenced harps
The worshippers left on the stairs.
I too have pain.

With each word he speaks,
As if words could break
Distant palaces apart,
The shadowy house
Before which Augustus sits
Crumbles onto its stairs.
Then the court becomes
A haunt of birds.
The law, merely a statement. Merely words.
His face merely a cast
The air had taken with a smothering
Handful of plaster at the moment
His illness took hold.

He sits in front of his house
With his hand held out,
Obeying the dictates of a dream,
Grown suddenly old.
Visible in the distance,
Behind his head, smoke issues
From the altars of Mars,
Venus, Saturn.
In the heart of diseased Rome,
Men hold buckets in the air
At the foot of smashed aqueducts.
Foreign deities are lumps of black ice
Beneath straw crowns,

Deities, skirted by nameless roads
Battered with hoofprints, who
Melt in the heavy rains—
The first Rome,
Dimly recalled from a soldier's
Drawing in the dirt,
Now up to its ankles in muddy lanes.

7

But Gabriel's blood foams in his chest.
He cannot bring himself to look.
This remnant of the bowl of reeling,
Stairways, the legendary well,
Back alleys, low doorways,
Even the starry regions overhead—
All are gravel, destined
To be recounted only in
The hidden alphabets,
In the metaphysical scrolls,
In other histories of other worlds;
But for now he turns away

To the woman
Who kneels before him
As if the light hurt, streaming
Into the broken room, who kneels
Like a marble subject begging
For her child's life in the reign
Of Augustus. He wavers
As if a gulf had opened up beneath him
In the dusty floor;
He is silent, as if in honor of one
About to die in a Roman war;
He wavers in the air
Above the place where he had stood,
Then he becomes
One of the pictures of holy streams
That flow in Joseph's hoard of wood.

8

Mary lifts her face from the deep
Shadows burying the floor, as if Azrael
With his shovel suddenly
Had knocked the ceiling in, and says:
Then open our empty tombs as well
On each of us.

SOLDIER ASLEEP AT THE TOMB

Piero della Francesca

In Palestine,
Where you are counting stars
To stay awake,
There is a legend that
The world was built
From nothing. There is a plaster crack
Ascending through the air
Above your head,
And you have laid aside
Your headgear
Covered with wolf skin,
But don't sink back,
Don't let your head
Tilt back, don't look up toward
The heaven's starry gulf and close your eyes,
Because you must not fall
Asleep. You must not sleep—
In Rome they crucified a dog
And carried it across
The city crucified upon its cross
Because once, long ago,
A dog in his old age
Slept through his watch,
And as he slept, the Gauls
Hoisted themselves in multiplying
Shadows across the brick
You lean your head on here—

You dream you run your palm across
A wall, and then, because
You must not fall asleep, you study it:

A map of enigmatic bricks
They manufactured in a city
Not located on the map,
With a thousand-thousand roads of mortar
Branching and rebranching
And, smiling from a pike
Before the gateway to the palace,
The head of a beheaded wolf
Tiberius once held up by the ears
And claimed was Rome,
Somehow become
A cap of wolf skin
You've retrieved
And laid in a sack
To carry on your shoulder,
Headed for Palestine—

You toil through mortar streets
Between the bricks
As if you knew the way,
But really you must admit
You're lost. But really
You must not lose the way.

As for that trench
Stretching before you
You dare not set your foot into that pit—
Rome is dried mud scattered into an opened
Artery. You must not drop away.
But then you do, you step away . . .
You step into a desert
Stretching out beyond
The outer city curb of Rome
To Palestine, where you are counting stars
To stay awake,
Where a legend in this region says
The world was built from nothing,

But these colossal walls
Adorned with hoists and pulleys,
These wheels and ropes
Hanging from scaffoldings,
Transform the temple complex
Into siege towers they rolled up to the base
Of a wall where now you crumble
A little mortar in your palm,
No more than twenty grains,
Crushed out of lime, sand, straw, gravel,
Marveling as if it were all that was left
Of Rome—
Rome must have worn away
Behind this wall, buckled without a sound.
A bank of mud where someone

Plunged a torch and left a crater
Lit now by your torch,
A reservoir so vast an army drowns
Struggling to get across,
Racehorses floundering in shipwreck
Over flooded circus floors

Toward mass graves dug behind the Esquiline
For Pompey's elephants
Who pleaded for their lives,
For persecuted bears,
For waterspouts of birds
Slain on the sand floor of the arena
One piercing blue afternoon,
Now become merely a stench
Behind a supporting wall,

Though, like a room turned inside out,
The wall spills over,
A petrified waterfall
Of sludge from the ancient wars
They waged on animals,
And elephants are nudging you awake because
You must not sleep.
You lift your head. You are outside.
You cannot surrender
Your sense that there is still an outside
Outside.

But when you look out the corner
Of your eye, the heaps of
Flamingo carcasses the soldiers carry
On sagging litters,
As if they had done battle
With the sunset,
Become a heap of murdered angels
Pitchforked from a horrifying height.
You are afraid to look
To your right.
Outside, the world
Is a hurled object.
The world is a stone sphere
That has rolled through
Other lives, and as it grinds past,
It trails a red stream.
There is an atrocious
Implication here.
So you lower your head,
Keeping your eyes
Closed, as if that way nothing
Will be disclosed.
But you must not fall asleep,
Not even leaning on your shovel for a moment—

The world was built from nothing,
Not with the strewn
Abandoned trowels they used
For sealing off a crime,

Not with a general's
Unmentionable treasures
The soldiers were unloading
In a mountain range of spoils,
Not with mountains of lime,
Of sand, straw, gravel, while the god
Who made the world
Looked on in his foreboding—

But all through the empire
They built this same
Slipshod maze of rooms
Tilting on shallow foundations
You were digging
With a shovel
Below, in frightful terraces,
A brickwork complex hemmed in by
Several succeeding outer stairs
Rumored to lead outdoors
Just as you awoke because

You must not sleep, no matter what.
No matter how cold the nail
Embedded in the ice
Of three o'clock,
No matter who orders you to impale
The wolf's head you've been
Arrested with,
Alone, in man-made landscapes

Built with force, beneath
The creak of timber bridges,
And then that complicated falling down
Of nonexistent walls beneath
A watchtower whose foundation could
Equally have served
To hold a sanctuary up,

Where you take
A narrow hallway to the right,
Skirting the wall along a narrow passage
To reach the courtyard
Of—a palace like a marble mountain
In whose throne room you approach
Tiberius from behind his chair,
And he turns around—

There is an execution
At the heart of it.
Then several successive waves of terror,
As well as marble
From that island in the sea
Of Marmara, marble dust
Like the miraculous snowfall
In August delineating
The shape of the basilica:
A cruciform snowprint—
You lower yourself over the side,
To drop to the next terrace and run.

But each time you arrive here,
Lifting your lamp,
You hear a sound.
You know your orders, after all.
Yet when you put your eye
To a chink in the wall
And try not to inhale
The nauseating taste of mud

You see distant, underground
Fires pouring toward you
For miles and miles,
Underground walls buckling inward
On towering labyrinths,
And a native angel trundling
A dog he's saved
In a straw wagon with clattering
Wooden wheels,
A dog who gives a bark
And sticks his nose
Through wooden slats
Against the angel's hand,
And cages of crucifixions, one by one,
Swaying above the heads
Of a group of distant soldiers;
But you step back,

You dream you run your palm
Across the wall, you dream

You guard an empty place
Where the plaster-crack ascending
Through the air above your face
Has multiplied,
As if a force behind the wall
Were pressing toward you
From the other side.

ANGELS GRIEVING OVER
THE DEAD CHRIST

The epitaphios of Thessaloniki

From those few famous silkworms smuggled
Into Constantinople in the head of a walking stick
Silk waterfalls
Poured from the ancient bolts

Into now-destitute reservoirs
Of church treasuries in Aachen,
In Liège, in Maastricht, in Sens,
In the Sancta Sanctorum of the Vatican,

Bright rivers seeping past
The age when a teaspoonful of
Silkworm eggs the size of one grain
Could endow a church,

The age when the letters in the words
Of sacred testaments were
Unreeled in the coastal cities of Asia Minor,
When a bookworm conspired

To wrest a maze of empty roads
Through the words *My Lord*—
That ancient, flickering text
Once permanently affixed

By blind but face-picturing, speechless
But law-breaking wooden shuttles,
Now a heap of gold wires displayed
With a crumbling silk vestment someone

Plucked from a shovelful of dust
During one of those treasure hunts conducted
In the burying grounds, in other eras,
A shovelful of dust

Now blowing into your eyes,
As if a storm wind from Paradise
Blew the rumors of this death
So hard you must cover your eyes

Before the museum case.
The late afternoon tugs
At a gold thread you can hear fraying
When you close your eyes,

A thread you feel your way along,
A thread at which the invisible globe pulls,
Leading you to the end of the world
Where there is a pile of

Clothes stolen from the grave,
Where your fear is relegated
To a masterwork of silk slaves—
That He is dead.

Here death is only a flash of worlds
Unfurled from a rifled
Church treasury, and you are invited
To walk this alluvial wave of gold,

To walk in the labyrinths
Of the angels' howls,
To run your hands along the walls
Of the silk thread's passageways,

To feel with your fingers
The angels' barbaric, stifled,
Glittering vowels
Tightly woven with gold wires.

If you were to tug at one,
Unraveling the angels
Into a vivid labyrinth of thread
From the fourteenth century

Backwards to the scissors blade
A seraph takes to a fragile
Filament of gilt
According to a law still unrevealed,

The shroud would disappear
In the gust of a little breeze
From this door left ajar
Into the next life,

The threshold we cross with closed eyes—
Where angels hide behind their backs
The saws with which they mean
To saw the present from the past,

Oblivious to the scarlet threads
That prove to be hidden among
The filaments, those red rivers
Running through the theme of time

So shockingly—so before you set foot there,
Take heed. This is the work
Of Byzantine silk slaves confined
To the palace grounds at Constantinople,

And you must beware.
There was a way station
On the Silk Road
Where the authorities executed

Traitors in a wooden box
In innumerable, unspeakable ways.
When you touch this shroud from the east
You take that hundred feet of road.

You must walk softly past.
You must try not to look.
The torrent of words—later, later.
Here tongues are cut out,

And that is why the howling
Is mute,
Gilded, herringboned.
Because although this is death,

It is the work of slaves
Whose task was only
To expose the maximum amount of gold thread
To the ceiling price of so many nomismata

Per square inch, in a swift mischief
Of curious knots, of mazes
Flashing past, of straight paths
Made inextricable,

So look again.
The angels wring their hands
Over a statue. They are deranged,
But not by grief. They mourn

Not a body, but a work in bronze.
They do not bring a mortal to the grave.
But we onlookers who grieve and grieve—
We cannot relegate this thought

To a glory woven cryptically
In heavy silks;
We cannot consign it, sweep it off,
For we cannot weigh

In our palms the empty cocoons,
We cannot study
Within the secret workshops
Of the silkworm,

We cannot touch the boiling
Water where the spools whirl,
We cannot learn firsthand
The bleakness of the craft

With which God made the world,
We cannot recount the legend that,
When they met face to face, both
God and the worm laughed.

CHRIST DEAD

Andrea Mantegna

I

Found among the painter's
Possessions at his death,
Something, of which one glimpse
Will wound your soul forever.

Something you seem to glimpse
Through intermediate planes of haze,
As if beyond overturned blocks
Of carved, square stone,
Something lying at rest,
Lying alone, even beyond
The nameless "uncarved block"—

As if you put your eye
To a chasm in the wall and beheld,
Through a caesura in the kingdom,
Through a space you cannot squeeze through,

The radiance of true exile
Where he lay in Sion a stumbling block
And a stone of offense, but here
Pictured in a perspective so narrow
You may only rest your forehead
On the ancient mortarwork
That holds you back from him.

So that, before this open tomb,
Pressing your face against the stone,
Seeing these lips that have touched

The bitter bread, halted
Before these wounded feet you cannot help
But reach for, as if you could
Take them in your hands,
You cannot refuse
To bow your head.

2

Andrea Mantegna meant this painting
For his own funerary monument,
To be placed by his heirs
At the foot of his coffin,
But instead, to pay his debts,
They sold it off
Into the ravenous inventory
Of Cardinal Sigismondo Gonzaga.

Back and forth, each day
For twenty years,
He paced the avenue between his house
And the ducal palace in Mantua—
The great avenue superimposed
By the little path that lay
Before him, the path through his days
To the end of his life,

Past workshop squabbles
And troubled relations with patrons
And lawsuits and false accusations,
Past easels with resurrections set
In the shadow-gardens
Of suburban residences of great families,
And curious drawings of recently
Unearthed antiquities
Seized for the collections of princes,
And designs for fountains, and ornamental scrollworks
In silverpoint and black chalk,

And gold cautiously ground into a powder
Measured out for gilt highlights
Trembling in mantles
Of pink watered silk,
And paper shapes wrought with scissors
For marveling onlookers,
And commissions for portraits
Of noble persons with riverscapes
Winding beyond palace windows—

But always ahead of him,
At the end of the path, this open tomb
That was not his.
Always with him until he died,
This rectangle of canvas
Propped on an easel in his house
In the upstairs room

Where, on September 13, 1506,
"At eighteen hours of the clock,"
He left behind his debts and cares,
He turned his back a last time
On his room above the street,
And began to toil up the side
Of Golgotha,
Where the cross, looming above,
Was empty now. No one was there.
And at the very end he bent to leave

Christ Dead behind,
Propped at the foot of the cross
Of his last breath.

3

Behind the little funeral procession
Winding down the slippery path,
The Roman soldiers turned away,
Gathered themselves, and fell
Into formation on the road—
Though one man twisted to look back
Over his shoulder several times,
Struck by something he couldn't say.

When he returned to Rome,
He heavily climbed the stairs
To the second story, to the same
Room where he had lived.
He unburdened himself,
Laying his sack aside on the same floor,
Setting his helmet down on the same table.
And, looking down into the lane
Of his old neighborhood below his room,
With his eye pressed to the cleft
In the wall, he saw, for himself,
The world he'd pined for in the east
Just as it was before he'd left.

TIBERIUS LEARNS
OF THE RESURRECTION

Eusebius, The History of the Church, *II, ii*

In a mock-Rome, built with bird cages,
The swallow was arrested for spying,
The pelican's beak was sawn off
For fishing a governor's pond without permission,

And a parrot, which made its entrance
In a covered basket, like a puppet-king
Carried in a litter who had recited
Upon his first glimpse of Rome

The lamentation of captivity
On behalf of those he had betrayed,
Now ignites into a dazzling green torch,
Crawling headfirst down

The wires against which, unfurling,
It momentarily crucifies itself,
Then folds into silence.
In a mock-Rome on the island,

The mirrors tilted against the corners
Of the ceiling are stifling,
Producing other worlds of angles
To spy on, showing, backwards

And forwards, an infinity
Of emperors, in a sequence of silvery rooms
Where the dagger-man leaps
But strikes someone else;

Where, strung up like withered cats
Who were executed for stalking
The talking birds from the thirty provinces
It is the Emperor's prerogative to strangle,

There are garlands for the Emperor,
The "Delight of the Human Race"—
Now nodding off, and sleep is a sheet of water
Glazing his troubled features. Tiberius

Dreams his face is carved onto
The front of a marble head,
Yet through his lowered eyes he sees
A little sparrow rolling toward his feet

A dry, round ball of straw—
His hand trembles outstretched before it,
For it may conceal the face of Drusus,
A faceless, featureless husk

Like a war trophy, a straw globe
Girdled with rope, a head with feathers
Where the mouth should be,
The mouth stuffed with mattress feathers

Owing to death by starvation, a head
Wrapped and sent to the Emperor
As proof of execution,
To whose lips he lowers his ear:

Man is a lamp that goes out when
I wave my hand. Man is a walking stick's
Ghostly supporter, following along.
Man is the victim of a wasp. A sack

Dragged to the Wailing Stairs and dropped.
A beggar's penny hurled into a well.
Something to wrap and bury in a hill.
Man is a madman clambering onto

The throne of Julius the God
At Augustalia, who picks up Caesar's crown
And puts it on his head, a crown
To crown the ruin of others with his own . . .

He tries to push it away,
But his bones weigh him down;
He sees his hand clatter down to his lap
Like a bone in an empty dish

And he cannot raise it; he tilts his head
And peers into a cistern, where,
Glinting at the bottom of a rumor,
Like a portrait of the Emperor,

An object's blinding brilliance
Makes him gasp himself awake before
The rim of, not a cistern, but
An orange blossom, offering not water

But an undrinkable perfume,
Like a pillow held to the face.
And mosquitoes float around his head
Forming soft, delicate, crazed

Letters in the air, writing his name,
Tiberius Julius Caesar Augustus,
A secret message of blame
He could crush into blood spots

If he could lift his hand.
Shoved around the island's boundaries,
The ocean's hurling-engines
Hurl bubbles into sand,

And banks of green-lit thunderheads
Are siege machines
Constructed in the Pax Romana,
Contraptions meant to terrify,

Lighting up a court of blue lizards
Like *agents provocateurs*
Pretending to cower among the frescoes
Of lemon trees

Though they are at the brink
Of showing their knives.
And a scribe
Is seated with his plume poised

Precisely on the last uttered letter,
A statue that writes,
These are my temples in your hearts,
These my fairest and abiding statues.

For those that are erected of stone,
If the judgment of posterity should turn
To hatred, are scorned
As sepulchres.

To be buried in one's own likeness
And image,
For a statue of one's self to be carried
By a slave through eternity,

A statue that crumbles, beginning with the face,
Into lime powder, to be carried
Past a flotilla of imperial barges,
Like water lilies, floating among

Courtiers, soldiers, scholars,
All of them corrupt. He climbs a mountainside,
Balding, bowlegged, to survey his quarries,
And a marble stairway, polished by flies,

Begins to revolve, a waterwheel
He is condemned to tread *in perpetua*,
Even when it crumbles beneath his steps
Into a flat ocean across which a slave

Walks toward him, whose lips are leprous
But he has bent to kiss . . .
His lips touch, inexplicably, flame.
A man laid in a new tomb,

Like a statue in the marble workshops,
But the eyes blindfolded,
The chin bound with gauze,
The statue of a god—of Tiberius,

Whose slaves carry statues of him
Down to the wharves, by the hundreds;
His features are multiplied in marble
A thousand times over, set afloat

On rafts, on ships, on imperial barges
Setting off, with carved blocks of marble,
Streaming past the rivers and ports
Into the open sea, the waterways

Filled with images
Of him, bound for marketplaces,
Temples, sacred crossroads,
Gardens, libraries,

His lips frozen, speechless among
The courtiers, the senators, the soldiers,
Unable to respond, to speak, to read
Aloud an inscription from which

His engraved name is stricken,
The marble face sheared off,
Exploding on the marble floor,
Or shipwrecked

In sand-laden winds,
In Egypt, where oceans are ponds,
In the reefs off Scylla,
In Greek underwater caves,

Where he somersaults slowly downward
Through an oceanic realm:
It is not the Roman custom
To condemn any man before

The accused meets the accuser
Face to face and has an opportunity
To defend himself
Against the charge.

He tries to lift his head,
A whited sepulchre
With his features; his stone hand
Lies across the scroll,

But where he had drawn a map
There is only a palsied star,
Like a wheel of knives wheeling
Toward him; he wrestles back

And starts awake. Nothing is there.
Mosquitoes softly float
Along a stone wall that conceals
A map embedded with borders of lightning,

And thunder rolls the sky away on wheels
Like a stone ceiling
Painted with clouds, but stone, stone.
Yet a god ascends through the worlds.

THE RESURRECTION

Piero della Francesca

In the 1550s a lantern maker, Marco, testified
That as a child he had "led Piero by the hand"
Through the streets of Borgo San Sepolcro.
Piero, blind, and following a child guide along

The chessboard of his native city's streets
To the Civic Palace, within the tumbled walls
Of the Town of the Holy Sepulchre. Piero, blind—
Who once, with earth imported from the Black Sea,

Had dusted pinhole pricks on tracing sheets,
To trace the *Dream of Constantine* on the wall,
And the serf who leaned against his shovel
Awaiting Helen's command to dig for the cross,

And Pilate, impassive, hooded in the Judgment Seat,
And the beautiful Jew who was tortured in a well—
Piero, white-gowned, a cataract prisoner, now
Shuffling, with outstretched hands, while far-off bales

Of straw, in fields ignited by the sunset,
Smolder behind him, setting a broken wall on fire.
The hem of a mantle of tree roots flames up
Like a patch of ancient sewing work littered

With those pearls for which Duke Federigo paid
A great price back in the old life, stitched
With silver leaf, in luminous embroiderings,
Lying tossed like a discarded shroud over

Kindling sticks in the hedge of thorns
The goldfinch once inhabited, her nest
A torch's head fallen from its stick
Beyond the curb of the marbly dream-town,

Where towers, knocked down across the countryside,
Half crumble like sugar-cube constructions
For a wedding, or dissolve like knocked-over
Buckets of sand for children's battlements—

For a city left behind in the wake of the earthquake
Of 1352, or the quake at Christ's death,
Since history is behind Piero now, and
The goldfinch is saved, circling ecstatically

Above Piero's head as he climbs a cement staircase
Step by step. *When you were young, you girded*
Yourself and walked wherever you would. But
When you are old, you will stretch forth

Your hands, and another will gird you,
And carry you where you would not go.
Halting in the streets of Holy Sepulchre,
Grown old in the town of his nativity,

Taken by the hand to the Civic Palace,
He stops at the site of *The Resurrection*,
And lifts his outstretched hand from Marco's shoulder,
As if he groped for the lip of a stone coffin

From antiquity set only inches away from where
The blind man appears to be staring in fright
Into God's face. Behind him the pink twinkle
Of twilight is a banner moist with one drop

Of Jewish blood; before him, the distant
Blue mountain of Purgatory. His fingertips touch
Only picture-shadowing earth from the Black Sea.
Once he could squint at *The Resurrection* through

An ever-smaller pinhole of light, like
A pinhole pecked for him by the finch's beak,
Through which he sifted powder for his drawings—
She whose nest had fallen when the mowers

Burned away the branches, she who had let
Piero approach, but only so far, and then
Warned him off with her gaze of terror,
When he would have bent on his knees in the grass

To stroke her anxious, silky head with
A fingertip, touching the scarlet cap
That stained it like a tiny, bloody drop,
But he'd backed away, not wanting to scare her—

But the pinhole he had peered through closed.
Now his shoes press against the plaster wall
Of blind old age, backed up by the empty place
Brick walls depict, where paint is a scent

That still could conjure the belfries of papier-mâché
He had painted for an important Duke,
A famous humanist he'd once depicted traveling
At twilight in a straw wagon with angels

Conversing in seraphic languages
Along the outskirts of a shining thunderstorm
Before the distant prospect of Rome–Jerusalem–Urbino.
Now he stands sightless with his empty hand

Outstretched at the rough edge of the sepulchre
Recently broken open, before which
Jesus has turned to Piero, holding out to him
Death's unraveled, pitiful bandages.

THE DREAM OF CONSTANTINE

Piero della Francesca

Long after the Messiah's men have entered
Every room in the city, and long after
Your government and seat of earthly power

Trudges far to the north, its army tents recentered
And sunk, like a meteor burned into the map,
This is the real end of the Roman Empire,

This storyless, this never-heard-of place
You find within, where there is only Constantine,
And vegetation, nudging the faces of boulders

. . . you saw rivers washing the very gates of the towns,
from the bend which leads the highway back toward Belgica,
you saw everything waste, uncultivated, neglected, silent,

shadowy—even military roads so broken that scarcely
half-filled, sometimes empty wagons cross them . . .
You gave us your whole life . . .

And there is a letter fallen out of the sky—
Through a window, far off in the distance,
They have drawn the dripping body of Maxentius

From the river and fixed his head on a pike,
To send it to Africa—but you dream an alphabet letter
Would shine beyond the borders of the New Rome, except

You had your men pry out and melt the bronze,
Leaving a chasm in the shape of a lightning-obliterated
Monogram, and there will come a time as well that,

Once you have laid your hands on the treasure
Of the nails that fastened His hands,
You will melt them into bridle bits and a helmet

And precious coins stamped with your portrait.
A letter fallen, a chunk of pediment, a stone
Carved from the fallen fragments of a dead moon

That turns out, when you examine it, to be
A meteor fragment with an engraved, ambiguous
Pockmark among other stones plunged into walled gardens

An empress studies in a miniature, circular
Hand mirror she holds over her shoulder, studying
Her hair, and the void at the heart of power

Where the senators don't speak Latin anymore,
Where barbarian horses clatter the cavalry stairs—
But when she turns around to look, Rome isn't there,

Only marble-carved studies of leaf-and-shadow
Floating above the entrance to gates
Long thought to be the handiwork of Greek slaves,

Crowned with orange blossom, and senators convene
To share their thoughts and turn to you,
But when you look through the gate you see

Nameless prisoners milling in a pig yard—
You lay down a law that the sacred precinct
May not be violated. No one may approach

The plot of ground you set aside, an orchard
Painted with bird cages for the Empress
And nightingales in flight and fountain jets

Raining parabolas of evaporating silver.
But as you approach, you see a figure
Strung up by the neck in the afterlife

Above the jawbone of an ass, clothes shredded,
While, in the background, Christ is beaten and bound.
The secret of the Empire was now disclosed:

That an emperor could be made elsewhere
Than at Rome. Other planets. Other laws.
Other hammers knock an alabaster sheet

Into a maze of cracks, a map of conquered districts,
New countries for the levying of the tax;
Other shovels are striking at an urn marked,

In the simplest imperial style, simply "Bones."
Your bones, Constantine, for in the end nothing
Could save you. But as for one's death, fixed into

The future like a stone that cries out in a wall,
It isn't now in any case, not at this moment.
There are churches to build, with spirits drawing

Compass points in the dust only steps ahead
Of Constantine, and letters to write to Jerusalem:
We wish this church to be the most beautiful in the world.

We have issued instructions to that effect
To the Vicarius Orientis, and the Governor of Palestine.
You awaken, in a tent on a field of battle.

Though your men boil grass to drink the water,
Though the moon flickers out—the battle is over
Long after the Messiah's men have entered

Every room in the city, and long after
Your engineers have affixed a pentacle
To the city and reported rumors of its miraculous

Founding, long after the dedicatory mosaic,
The visual liturgy, the setting for a crisis
In gold glass, monophysite particles swimming upward

Out of the prisons of ecclesiastical geography,
Escaping when everything must be included,
Escaping when nothing must escape, not even dust,

For history is either a prison, a repository belonging
To the victorious Emperor, or else a patch of snow
A group of kneeling slaves hammers and hammers—

Let them hammer the heads of their own shadows.
You will win the battle. The city of Rome is yours,
And never mind the rumors thronging your ears

Like angels pouring along a map of black roads
Through the mosaic's gold squares, angels rushing
Toward you through the labyrinths of mortar

From other capitals with other crucifixions
At the ends of other lanes, dimly beheld
In cities that have yet to be founded,

At whose outskirts other emperors sleep in their tents.
For now there is you at the picture's center.
And never mind the angels thronging your ears

With rumors of lamps up ahead that refuse
To stay lit for your armies, with rumors
That no lamps are lit in the cities your armies enter.

PART THREE

A MONUMENT

IN UTOPIA

A MONUMENT IN UTOPIA

(Osip Mandelstam)

When a word is spoken in the name
of its speaker, his lips move in the grave.
—*Talmud, Tractat Yevamot, 97a*

I

In a time when poetry will be filled
With a peripheral fleet of swans
Glimpsed in the heavy, carved mirrors
That bring the willow park
With its long, statue-ringed, green ponds
Through the windowpane
Into the drawing room
So that, even standing inside,
We seem to look outdoors
Into a room of green rain;

In a time when poetry will no longer
Be a door fallen open upon
A dangerous conversation,
A door pushed shut in the Iron Age
Upon topics better saved for the open streets
And that famous glance
Over the shoulder,

Topics gliding over your life and mine,
But lighting upon the destiny of one
Who escaped to Paris;
In a time when, once having spoken,
A man will be allowed
Simply to resume growing older;

Then a notebook may be allowed to lie
Abandoned on the outer stairway,
Its pages turning freely back and forth
In the breeze, as if a spirit were reading,

And winter will come
Together with headlines in the *Herald*
Announcing that this season
Everyone in the city is mad for pearls,

Then a lost world will be only as trivial
And only as panic-engendering
As a lost pearl
That has rolled under the bed,
And, like all domestic artifacts
In this age, will be easily retrieved again—
Then the word *impearled*
Will no longer give way to the word *imperiled,*
Not even for you, who disdained to twist
Rhymes apart with a knife for their pearls—

And through the streets of the city, the cold pink cliff
Of afternoon's glacier will press its path,
Dropping at its forefront the crumbling
Particles of twilight's mauve, pushing past
The momentarily lustrous *glass panes*
Of eternity where you had laid
The humid whorls of childhood's breath.

No one will be under arrest;
The enlightenment will be behind us;
When we hurry past the metropolitan library
No one will look out at us in fright
From the top of his cast-off overcoat,
No one will reach from his orphan's sleeve
With a child's yearning hand
Trapped in the rising waters of the age,
No features hauntingly difficult to place
Will perch precariously on a throat
As gaunt as a starved pencil.
And the vexing labyrinths
Of injury and debt will have plunged away
Together with the false testimony of
Bad neighbors and ungrateful friends;
No one will scrawl a message that ends
If I can just get through these years . . .

And surging away, far behind us,
That purge of down-at-the-heels cosmopolitans
Will be swallowed up
Together with our recollection
That these mammoth canals
And cavernous buildings were built
With the labor of prisoners like you
Back when the uprisings meant
That men rose up to dispose
Of their next-door neighbors.

Even if the avenues will be mobbed
With former prisoners from that time,
A non-person will be free to survive the winter,
To observe, from the comfort of his own coat,
His native city by lamplight
Along the black ice of the frozen river,
With its frilly crust
Of half-lit, golden snow
Like a mille-feuilles
Glimmering with apricot glaze
And ready to crumble beneath the tooth,
Whose sugar grains melt on his tongue—

He will be free to look into a succession
Of snowflakes poised on his glove
As if he had idly lifted a kaleidoscope
To his eye and seen street maps
Of harmless utopias succeed one another
In a swift, geometrical blaze,
Like hypothetical maps
Of a village you once passed through,
Though functionaries have made a point
Of sealing off those documents
That mention you.

Back then, the heavenly axle tree,
Like that verse about the sound the earth makes
As it rotates on its invisible axis
In a breathless rhyme with your name,

Was only a set of revolving doors
Swooping into a marble office building,
Constructed and installed
By means left unrecorded,
Where a malicious servant of the state—
Who, after all, was a non-person too,
Whose teeth doubtless pained him,
Whose backstairs doubtless smelled of ammonia—
Was seated at his desk in 1937,
Before seventy speeches, a blizzard of papers,
Correspondence witnessed under
Dread of death, and documents leading to a man
Pushing a wheelbarrow of stones
Along a path near Vladivostok, as if
Illustrating an axiom as yet unpropounded.
He blotted with a tissue the fresh ink
Where his signature stained the document,
Tamping his name, as if he tried to arrest
A seepage of blood:

A sphere has squeezed itself into my room,
Backing me against the wall of my office—

What is it! The New World escaped from a pen,
The substitute world we designed

To put an end to suffering and doubt,
Though once it did loll and roll about

Above the most poverty-stricken and threaten
To explode—soap!—

A hollow, wobbling, flashing sphere
But not this hardened monoglobe

Rolling out of the palace
Of the nineteenth century

I thought the ages rolled away from us
Not toward us

I first heard it
Rolling through a word,

A word like a bubble fleeing,
But a bubble growing

Until it rolls through the streets, it rolls up
To the door of my office and squeezes through—

Oh, the world is rounder in Red Square
Than it is anywhere—

If I slash it with my scissors,
I see my shadow on its surface

If I stab it with my pen,
If I take a hammer to it—but the stains,

If it should burst, the horrid stains,
Oh, worlds, worlds are dashing in my brains!

2

Even if war should rattle
That window on Europe again
Beyond the mahogany dining table
Shined into a dark-brown mirror,
The silver inkwell picked up at an auction
Gleams on its stand
Like an ornate wishing well,
A well no longer brimming
With the ice-crowned black water
Toward which the Grand Princes were lowered,
But only with a spray of heavy roses
Sipping transparent water,

An inkwell that once belonged
To Victor Hugo,
Who, as he lifted and stroked
His beard like a mantle of
Century-old wisteria, had declared
That torture was at an end
Around the world, and had raised
His glass to that thought—

Even if war should rattle that window again,
Now the fall
Of the Second Empire is no more
Momentous than currency changing hands
At a distant border, though
Mixed with some reports of war,

And rumors of revolution mean
Only that there will be time
For uninterrupted study
At the once desolate kingdom
Of your desk, where you may escape
Everything and everybody,
Where the only thing you surrender to
Is a paper world, where error may be rectified
With a single pencil stroke
And no one is hurt,
Where among the reams of blank paper,
And the rules of the pencil
With its featureless, annihilating eraser,
You are at liberty to lower your ear
To the verse of an ancient eclogue

Where the house of the bee
Is enlarged by another room,
Held fast with fragrant wax,
And, nearer and nearer,
The humming workers thresh the air
Charged with their labor's mysterious joy,

And snails sway on little stems,
Lost in a meditative slumber
As morning opens up a box
Of heavenly blessings without number.
You hear a girl's foaming hems

Churn a wake of white, blue-eyed grasses—
She carries her flower scissors open
To shear the locks
Of the heaped-up lilac branches
Leaning like tinted sheep
Against a fence that sags beyond repair,
As a cream-yellow, infant cabbage moth
Blunders into her hair—

You could reach your hand
Into the tendrils along the nape
Of the sweet peas exhaling on the trellis,
Of the rose mallow, the may apple, the fox grape,
In the century of carelessness at piano lessons,
Of embroidered alphabet letters,
Of paper prisons for crickets,
Of pulling wooden swans on strings—
Of coming face to face with
The surprising beetle at the foot
Of the blade of grass, whose mandibles
Revolve at the foundations
Of your memory,

Until the only revolution
You can follow any longer
Is day revolving into night, as silently
As leaves alternating with shadows
In black and white on a balcony—nothing more,

And rumors mean only that you seize
The chance to abandon your book,
Though successive new worlds roll
With a great force over the floors
Of your era, staining our ceilings
In that apartment where we still are frozen,
Where we still flash our eyes
Past the lists of the accused,
We still find our families' names
Scribbled into the margins
In an unfamiliar hand—
Where, even without you, we still stand
At the window and stare *into the frost's face.*

But you loved the winter because it was
"The one thing they could not take away"
Even after that night the end appeared
As a broken window, after the war
That landed on the wall of your apartment
Like a falling star—except
That apartment had only ever existed on paper,
And paper was the first thing
They would take away.

3

And that bookcase from your childhood—
Never to be recovered, of course—
That bookcase your parents moved
From one apartment to the next,
From Maximilian Lane to
Ofitserskaja Street and Zagorodnyj Prospekt,
The one you saved, and saved, and saved,
And *then* lost

As you fled the ravine that opened up
Between two revolutions
While families peeped from basement windows
Along one of those black boulevards
We see in the peripheries of
A glass of boiled water
At whose rim you sniffed the lead pipes
Of waterworks from the Golden Age—

Your childhood encyclopedia
With those names that had not yet begun
To boil on the maps,
And the gilt-edged Bible's
Whiff of smoking Paradise
Among the gutted Hebrew letters,

And the flattened hemispheres
With the seven blue oceans
You had thumbed threadbare,
Your schoolboy Herzen

With your scribbled drawing
Of a man seated at the base of the "wall
Which cannot be destroyed,"

Your Hans Christian Andersen's
Nightingale, where there is a courtier
Of such importance that, when a man
Of lower rank dares to ask him a question,
He habitually answers only "P,"
Which means nothing at all;

And Baudelaire, Hugo, Lamartine,
The choices of a French governess,
And notebooks where everything
You penciled into the margins has smeared
Like the pain-blunted words you searched for—
Supposedly easily retrieved—
In the throbbing labyrinths
Of a cigarette ember, in the remotest
Reaches of migraine, the margins
Where you had copied out
Something from Aristotle, because he broke

Words into syllables,
Then into letters: the word PERSON,
If it was broken into P and E and R,
Still would shed no blood, would expose
Nothing that would make us dizzy.
Beyond the disintegration of a word

A string of letters simply floats away—
And beyond the disintegration of a letter
There floats a silence so absolute
That, presumably, there is nothing left to say,

Not even in your turn-of-the-century
"Illegally suppressed"
Editions that weighed so much
They bowed the shelf and it threatened to snap,
The way other bookshelves in other countries
Have sagged with an additional fact
Since the date of your arrest.

Those books, dumped out,
Are still drifting down somewhere between
The autumn of 1900
And the later fortunes of a region
That hurled itself into a terrifying dream;
They still are falling through the air,
Still fluttering out across the century
And have not hit bottom,

Nor has that trunkful
Of worthless paper money
From the time of Nicholas the Second—
Pathetic money, stuffed behind
Miniature embroideries of your native city's
Colossal neoclassical boulevards
Built with forced labor
And depicted on frivolous cushions;

Money, shaken from the pages of novels,
Fluttering down through the air of an apartment
Where papers are sewn into pillows,
Or into the linings of coats,
Or stuffed into shoes,

With papers that fluttered out of your sleeve
On the night of your arrest,
And drifted over Europe,
Landing here, on a library shelf;

Money, no longer stamped, like the odes
From that period, with the cheap,
Benevolent portraits of monsters,
No longer giving off an acrid scent
As if a frightened man had touched it,
No longer with torn edges unraveled
Into a plush hedge the chief police interrogator
Runs his thumb along, before he crumples the bills
One by one into paper spheres, and wades
Among skittering ghost-worlds,
On his way out the door, his ankles
Brushing against wads of paper
That once upon a time
Could have bought you a coat.

5

Five thousand miles east of *childless Petrograd,*
You! You, with your hair-raising tales,
Your coat without buttons, your raging fits,
Your history of poverty, your torn cigarettes!
You, with your heart still set
On impossible things,
Touching the top of your head absently
Like the Pharaoh's baker trying to explain
His dream that there were birds
Devouring cakes from a basket on his head—
Then falling silent to feast upon a grain of sugar
That audibly melted on your tongue,
A crumb you lifted to your lips
With a delicate finger-and-thumb
In a trance of concentration,
The first grain from that half kilo of sugar
Like a sack of diamonds finely ground
For which you traded a shredded
Yellow leather overcoat in December,
Though God knows where you'd acquired
Such a coat,

Though granted that, in the old stories,
Garments are lavished on paupers;
Granted that, in one's childhood books,
The coat of the King
Always comes to rest around
The stooped shoulders of his poorest subject,
Albeit no longer lined with a flash of silk,

No longer even held together
With the precious stitches of silk thread

Inside the coat of Akaky Akakevich,
Who, though he squandered all that he had
For his lofty dream of a new overcoat,
Though for months he went hungry at night,
Though he did without tea and candles,
Still had to skimp on the calico lining
And a collar of cat's fur.

Even at the Expulsion, God made
With His own hands garments of fur and skin
For the expelled—

But for you the sum of your inheritance,
Of which you were robbed anyway,
Was a veil of threads handed down
Through the generations, a veil descended
From that succession of stolen overcoats
Stuffed with paper shreds
From the nineteenth century.

Out there a giant scissors pursues
Little men, insignificant men, non-persons,
Up and down the lanes of Vtoraya Rechka,
Clacking and clacking behind them,
Cutting their overcoats into streamers,
Until all that is left is a bit to drape

Over the shoulders, but not enough
To cover the face with, when the time comes.

And who wouldn't want to press
His coat on you?
Who wouldn't exchange
Your bunk for his comfortable bed?

Who, then, that has lived such a life
Has escaped the Emperor's notice?
For each and every one of them
Was denounced.
What land and sea did he not thoroughly search,
What clefts in the rocks,
What secret holes in the earth,
That he might bring to the light of day
One who was hidden there? And once he had found
Such a one, he would carry him away,
And not to his palace, either.

You will be free to wander
In the metropolitan library,
Free to stare,
Without arousing suspicion,
At the statue voted by the senate
To honor Poetry,
Once a block of undifferentiated marble
Originally destined, in the old life,
For a grandiloquent hotel lobby
In the Empire style, hinting at transports
Of stone in wobbling wheelbarrows driven
Along filthy lanes by men whose fingernails
Are suitable for decapitating fleas
And scratching their beards as if
They sandpapered a shadow—
Once a block of marble,
Yet now a spirit glinting in the room,
With a starry hoard of words
Like tiny prisms on its lips.

Although the rhapsodes themselves
Will be banished from the reading rooms
To the public park, exiles
Even from the reconstructed life,
Framed in the library's windows,
They will reappear in bronze
Along the radiating paths,
Among the avenues of limes, for miles;
They will populate the gravel walks

In greatcoats, holding hats and books,
Although with interchangeable heads
In deference to changing tastes and styles.
Among the reveries of oval ponds
Like looking-glasses with drifting swans,
None will be represented pushing a wheelbarrow,
No man, with his head between his knees,
Will be seated and puking between his feet,
No scarecrow with his hands
Fastened beneath his armpits,
Looking cautiously over his shoulder
From his gravel mound,
Will thus indicate the wind-chill factor
On the "date of death unknown."

Seated in the shade of your monument,
Where you will wear an absurd morning coat
Far above your station in life,
Schoolboys will read your lines:
Now I'm dead in the grave with my lips moving
And every schoolboy repeating the words by heart.
Although you are laid nowhere in a grave,
Although you speak without moving your lips,
Although your words shine by themselves.

Beyond the statues of Important Persons
Posthumously rehabilitated,
Retired prison guards will be seated in the shade
In flocks along the banks of a green river

As if a goosegirl had driven
Them to the edge of the pond.
Seated on stone benches,
They will be excused, and pensioned off;
In their eighties now, they will snooze
And nurse their tea, and their frail shoulders
Will shake when they cough.
At night, for them, there will be
A tincture of valerian and a teaspoon
Glimmering on the bedside table.

Even that one will have attained
A gentle expression
Who stirred the gravel with a stick
And asked, *So now where is your poetry?*
Even his shadow will tower over nothing more
Than a board of dominoes,
His double chin propped on his fist,
His elbow crushing wadded headlines.

He will die in his own bed
Like an old woman, his head dropping down
Between his glass of tea and a needlepoint cushion
Where a tattered finch flutters,
Though it is stabbed to the heart,
Across a shallow autumnal stream
Plush with once-bright-red thread
Gone muddy brown;

For him, death will lie
Open like a newspaper in a dream,
A paper he ransacks his apartment for,
And when he lays his hands on it at last,
As he smooths the crinkled page to read,
He will simply spread before his face
Not a page but, oddly, a black comet,
Or rather a rococo ornament in empty space
Hanging intriguingly before his eyes,

And he will turn his face toward an evening
So thick with butterflies
Along a blurry road
That the convoy truck in which he is transported
Will lay two black tire stripes
Through the white, rustling millions . . .

It will have evaporated,
That whiff of the scaffold, the siege tower,
Of vaults sealed so long that no one
Would wish to break them,
That sense that a bone is being broken
Somewhere in the world,
That one's number is called out.

Even the dictator, the son of a devout
Washerwoman and a cobbler who savagely beat him,
Will be seated in the library among
Unsuspecting readers,

Including you, where you will be hidden
Behind your book, thumbing the last page
Of your life, still afraid to read it;

Even the dictator will leave off
Doodling wolves in red ink,
And will begin, tentatively, to explore
The vaults of white paper
With a sharpened pencil,
Where howls still will be trapped
In the gray zone of lead;
Even he will turn a sequence of the intricate
Misfortunes of other people
Into icy, twinkling, jagged meters
Until the page will be as blackened
As those black wells
Into which you were lowered
In a nightmare of the skull-piled woods
Outside of Novgorod:

The world is a closed and unique system,
A monoglobe, a monument to permanence,
With one center and a limited circumference,
A manifest point to exile others from,

To banish the vanishing point once and for all,
After we've swept the past into it and shut
The lid. There is no point outside the world
Which cannot be destroyed. And the world is small—

We may measure it, in inches, with calipers,
On a sheet of paper, and calculate its weight.
We may whirl the pencil around and around
The needle that bores a hole in the paper's center

Into the lives of others. There are no others;
Others are us; and we have covered sinkholes
And graves and regions of war with paper
On which it is written and signed that we are brothers:

Here history begins. As for that creature
Cowering in the corner, he is one we found
On the other side of the paper wall
When we began to bore a hole in the world—

Pay no attention. We approach the hour
Without populations of rebels, without synagogues
Of doodling devils, there will be no jails
Once we have emptied them and we will scour

The prison walls before we close them forever.
No matter what blood spattered on our shoes,
Whatever lives lie crumpled at our feet,
We'll roll the globe before us with a lever,

We'll prove beyond a doubt the world is man's,
A monument to us, a monoglobe
With a manifest point and a limited circumference,
And it never can fall into the wrong hands.

7

If I could begin again,
Time is something I would measure
In the generations of roses, evolving across
Gulfs we have no records of,
Eons without archives,
Eras without witnesses,
Without surviving portraits,

Roses flowering past the cliffs
Of thirty million years
Without intent,
In galaxies of tints,
In repetitious, variegated depths
Above the sinkholes of our wars,
Our vanishing points,
With hints
Portrayed in velvet;

If I could begin again,
I would measure time in the generations of
Roses, and not the succession
Of rulers of men,

In that fragrant clambering
Across the cliffs between millennia,
In the world without us,
Roses linking their chains among outcroppings
Of stone and shale
High overhead or drifting

To the bottom of twenty dozen centuries
Or oversprawling, on their jagged stems,
Chaos—

To never wonder what they meant,
To never envision
Nero's face again,
Though roses were destined
To be his favorites,
Fluttering from his ceiling,
One of the varieties of damask rose
Killed off, they say,
By the eruption at Pompeii,
Depicted on the walls of plastered bricks,
Unscented as music, and
The gallica roses, established
After the fall of Rome wherever
They had fallen,
They never asked themselves
Whether it was worthwhile
To save the Roman Empire
In order to make it a vast prison
For scores of millions of men.

Though here
The Latin library crumbles,
The archives tumble, the Tabularium
Buckles into a rose garden
Where we piled texts from centuries

In cliffs of commentaries
While nature was tracing out her beauties
In the medium of flower-flesh,
Building her roadways
Out of haze,
Her repositories out of snow
Whether thirty million years ago
Or here and now

Where the year of your death
Rolls up to the foot
Of Stalin as if he could give orders
For the years to come and go,
As if he could decree
That not a single green leaf
Is to be left on the branches,
That each growing leaf
From the old world
Is to be repressed,
Nothing is to be left,
Though his secretary
Will scissor roses away
To set on the great man's desk,
In Utopia, when he will rest from his wars—

But there, where roses press ahead,
There the boundaries are vague,
The numbers of their species
Are disputed, each new leaf

Unfurls and grows
In time's sidereal gulfs
Toward other flowerings,
Other unfurlings, other
Floatings toward a very different future
Rose by rose,
Flowering above
Brick walls whose foundations
Are shattered statues
Wedged into the foundations of bad dreams
Our flashlights scan,
A jumbled perpetual night of broken pieces,
Of frozen motion and sagging seams,
Pressing through a rift in time,

Flowering past that mound of heads
At Utopia's borders,
Composed of portraits of
The heads of households,
Of beloved daughters, blind rhapsodists,
Of gods reduced to begging with
Their delicate hands held out midair,
Marble arms and legs akimbo in frozen rape,
Masterpieces ground down for ballast,

Even when we pass the torch
Of our holocaust near their petals,
They instantly parch into irretrievable
Miniature scrolls we cannot excavate,

A speechlessness
With nothing to lament,
Uttering nothing even for the one
Whose face we know
Amid the blind roots of trees
In an apple orchard, in the loam
Of centuries of rubbish, jammed up
To the hilt in mud and snow,
In the generations
Of roses flowering past a group of graves
We have never visited,
Graves we haven't known of,

Above which pink-golds, rose-golds, gold-reds
Are evolving, with nothing in mind,
The tints that make their way
So wordlessly, millions
Mutating into vermilions, flowering past
The established *annus mundi*
Written into rock
In 49 at Antioch,
At Gaza in 61,
At Alexandria in 30,
Bostra in 106—

Clambering past borders
And successions of years, with
Multileveled, multipetaled realities
Reaching beyond our eventual absences

For resurrections expressed without
Faith or doubt,
Compared to which our lives and histories,
Our moral wanderings,
The history of our disgrace,
Are merely a crumpled disorder
To shovel over,

Merely pages to tear from
Childhood's classic picture books,
Where, among the formal gardens,
The little figures of Redouté and Josephine
Bend to the easels:

He is teaching the art of flower painting
To a queen
To celebrate their bloodless beheadings,
And at their backs
Bushels of roses heaped along the fence
Disappear along hazy roads
In districts we no longer stroll,
Among what overgrowings,
What loiterings on trellises,
What comings and goings
In other people's childhoods,

The roses' silence unbroken,
Piled high in wagons like
Captives bound for the metropolis,

Trundling past each century,
The favorites of Nero,
The possessions of Constantine,
The emblems of Saladin,
Flowering toward a time when there is no
Nero, no anti-Nero,
No Constantine, no Saladin,
But only roses on their paths
To someplace else,
Some other point of rest,

Flowering past our multitudes
Of local eras, our eschatologies,
Our beginnings and ends,
Our indictions, our "destinies of kingdoms,"
Our fifteen-year cycles, our holy days
And warring calendars,
Our Era of Martyrs,

Flowering past the fence
Above our death dates hidden even
From the angels—
Transitory monuments
Pouring out their whorls,
Piling up their treasure heedlessly
In the vaults of air.

REFERENCES

Part One / A Gilded Lapse of Time

Phrases from Dante's *Comedy* are drawn variously from translations
by John Ciardi (New York: Mentor, 1970), Allen Mandelbaum
(New York: Bantam, 1984), and John D. Sinclair (Oxford:
Oxford University Press, 1939).

Phrases from St. Augustine's *Confessions* are taken from translations
by R. S. Pine-Coffin (Baltimore: Penguin, 1961), Rex Warner
(New York: New American Library, Mentor-Omega, 1963), and
Eugene TeSelle in "Augustine," in *An Introduction to the Medieval
Mystics*, edited by Paul Szarmach (Albany: State University of
New York Press, 1984).

I

when you hear your name: This is an adaptation of a folk superstition
described, by Nikolai Gogol, in *Old-World Landowners*, as a
prophecy of one's own imminent death.

bees who had laid aside: In Isaiah 7:18–19, following the prophecy of
the Messiah, God whistles for the bees to come out of the land
of Assyria.

unfinished combs: In I Samuel 14:24–29, the Israelites are faint with
hunger, and in the woods they have found a honeycomb that
drips on the ground; but Saul has forbidden them to eat. Only
Jonathan has not heard his father's interdiction: "wherefore he
put forth the end of the rod that was in his hand, and dipped
it in an honeycomb, and put his hand to his mouth: and his
eyes were enlightened."

In classical antiquity, bees and honey were associated with poets and
poetry-making, as in Plato's *Ion*, and with gifts of divination,
prophecy, song, eloquence, and truth-telling. Bees were thought

to embody the souls of the dead, as in Aeneas' vision of underworld souls destined for reincarnation in the *Aeneid*, VI, 703; it was thought they could impart gifts of poetry to those whose lips they touched with honey, as in the epitaph by Antipater of Sidon on Pindar in the *Greek Anthology*, VII, 34, and in some instances the bees were said even to have built a honeycomb on the poet's mouth. In Latin poetry, this legend frequently is expressed explicitly, for example, in Horace's "Ego apis Matinae," and implicitly, for example, in Virgil's associating of Orpheus with Aristaeus, the first beekeeper, in Book IV of the *Georgics*.

2

God repented after He made man: Genesis 6:6: "And it repented the Lord that he had made man on the earth, and it grieved him at his heart."

those vessels God had wanted to use: The "breaking of the vessels," also known as "the death of the primordial kings," is a kabalistic Jewish creation legend, suggested in the Zohar and famously elaborated by Isaac Luria. The version of the legend quoted here is recounted by Gershom Scholem in an essay entitled "Sin and Punishment."

3

In the *Trattatello in laude di Dante*, Boccaccio, on the authority of Dante's friend Piero di Giardino, writes that Dante had hidden away the last thirteen cantos of *Paradiso* before embarking on a journey to Venice that proved fatal to him. After his sudden death, the ending of *Paradiso* was considered lost. Dante's sons attempted to finish the poem themselves. Eight months after Dante's death, his son Jacopo dreamed that Dante appeared to him and led him to the room where the last cantos were hidden behind a mat pasted to the wall next to the bed where Dante had died. When Jacopo awakened from the dream, he hurried to the house of Piero di Giardino to rouse him, and the two men hastened to the room where Dante had died; there they discovered the cantos in the location described in the dream. The verses were in a dangerously deteriorated condition from the damp mold of the wall, but they still were legible enough for Jacopo to make a copy of them.

4

The fountains also of the deep . . . : Genesis 7:11.

6

We are water: II Samuel 14:14: "We are like water that is spilt on the ground."

7

The speculation that the concentric spheres must exist is quoted from Theon of Smyrna, *Expositio rerum mathematicarum ad legendum Platonem utilium*, translated by S. Sambursky in *The Physical World of Late Antiquity* (Princeton: Princeton University Press, 1962).

8

There is no depiction of God the Father in the mosaics in San Vitale, except for the image of the divine hand reaching down from heaven to withhold Abraham's hand from the sacrifice of Isaac. The Messiah is portrayed both as a beardless youth enthroned on a celestial sphere in the apse, from which the four mystical rivers pour, and as the risen Redeemer in a medallion at the center of the interior vault leading toward the apse.

the creation was subjected: Paul writes "the creation was subjected to vanity" in Romans 8:20.

marble caterpillars: In *Purgatory*, X, 124–26, Dante describes the human soul:

> . . . *do you not know that we are worms and born*
> *to form the angelic butterfly that soars,*
> *without defences, to confront His judgement?*
>
> *(tr. A. Mandelbaum)*

a holy stream: Circulating throughout the *Comedy* are numerous metaphors portraying God as a miraculous source of water, a fountain, a river, a spring, an ocean, a heavenly raining. In *Paradiso*, XXX, 88–89, Dante dips his face into a river of light and lets it cascade from his eyelashes. Dante is thought to have died of a malarial fever he contracted in the marshlands between Ravenna and Venice.

Ephphatha: In Mark 7:34, Jesus utters the untranslated Hebrew word *Ephphatha* in healing a man of two ailments simultaneously: deafness and impaired speech.

The authenticity of Dante's death mask, which was not discovered until centuries after his death, is disputed.

That wound, inflicted inadvertently: In Canto XIII of the *Inferno*, in the Wood of the Suicides, Dante is struck dumb with pity and fear when, at Virgil's urging, he hesitantly tears a little branch away from a thorn tree and the tree shrieks in pain; words and blood issue out simultaneously. Dante discovers, in this terrible way, that the thorn trees in this desolate wood are the transformed souls of human suicides, who are enabled to speak only in the medium of blood, and only as a result of injury. Dante draws this moment from a similar incident between Aeneas and the soul of Polydorus in the *Aeneid*.

17

A bell at the Dante Museum in Ravenna, next to Dante's Tomb, rings thirteen times at dusk in memory of Dante's homesick recollection of the Compline bell in *Purgatory*, VIII, 1–6.

18

Whose movement is swift . . . : In *Convivio*, II, iii; and Dante's speculation that without the movement of the primum mobile the planet Saturn would be hidden from earth for fourteen and a half years, the planet Jupiter for six, and the planet Mars for nearly a year, is recorded in *Convivio*, II, xiv, translated by Patrick Boyde in *Dante Philomythes and Philosopher* (New York: Cambridge University Press, 1981).

She had lived: Dante's astronomical calculation of the length of Beatrice's life is recorded in *La Vita Nuova*, I, ii, translated by Barbara Reynolds (New York: Penguin, 1969).

19

to fix it in my sight: As he approaches the brilliant Sphere of the Sun, Dante asks the reader to "lift your eyes with me to see the high wheels," as translated by Allen Mandelbaum, or to "raise your eyes across the starry sphere," as translated by John Ciardi, in *Paradiso*, X, 7–8, in order to regard the point of the vernal equinox as the mark of the perfection of God's art; and he says in line 12 of the same canto that this is a picture which God, out of love, has "fixed forever in His sight" (tr. Ciardi).

Part Two / Crux of Radiance

2

The ambitious building activities of Herod the Great, who rebuilt the Second Temple, are described by Josephus in *The Jewish War*, I, 401.

4

Some details of the capture of the people in the first stanza are taken both from Thucydides' description of the captured Athenians in Sicily in *The Peloponnesian War* and from Josephus' description of the destruction of Jerusalem in *The Jewish War*.

5

The description of the end of days in lines 4–7 is from Ecclesiastes 12:3–7.

All the knives were reground . . . : Adapted from rules, in the Babylonian Talmud, Tractat Avodah Zarah, 49b and 76b, concerning the purification of knives and the destruction of pottery (in fulfilling the requirements of kashrut), and the destruction of fabric woven with implements made from wood associated with idols.

6

Suetonius reports in *Augustus*, XCI, that once a year Augustus would sit before his house on the Palatine, with his hand outstretched, begging for coins, in obeyance of a dream he had once had.

SOLDIER ASLEEP AT THE TOMB

The portrait of the sleeping soldier who faces the viewer in Piero della Francesca's *Resurrection* (c. 1458) in the Civic Palace at Borgo San Sepolcro is said, by Vasari, to be Piero's self-portrait.

Livy recounts in his *History of Rome*, V, xlvii, the legend of the Gauls' assault "one starlit night" on the Capitoline. The Gauls climbed the walls so silently that the watchdogs were not awakened, but the noisy geese, sacred to Juno, awakened the soldiers. The birds were celebrated for having saved Rome.

a beheaded wolf: Suetonius, in *Tiberius*, XXV, records that Tiberius said that in ruling Rome he was holding a wolf by the ears.

ANGELS GRIEVING OVER THE DEAD CHRIST

The title is from a description of the Thessalonikan epitaphios in *Byzantium*, by Paul Hetherington and Werner Forman (London: Orbis, 1983). Hetherington proposes that the epitaphios, an orthodox liturgical length of cloth, was worn, perhaps, over the heads of priests as they approached the altar to celebrate the Eucharist. The epitaphios of Thessaloniki was discovered in 1900.

both God and the worm laughed: I have not been able to locate the source of this legend.

CHRIST DEAD

Mantegna's legendary painting, now in the Brera Gallery in Milan, is variously dated from 1457 to 1500. Although monumental in character and feeling, the painting measures only 68 × 81 cm.

"uncarved block": The source for this image is *The Tao Te Ching* of Lao-Tzu, as translated by Arthur Waley (New York: Grove Press, 1958).

he lay in Sion: Romans 9:33: "I lay in Sion a stumblingstone and rock of offense."

Eusebius records the extraordinary legend, first recounted by Tertullian, that the Emperor Tiberius heard news of the Crucifixion and Resurrection of Jesus in Palestine, that Tiberius was favorably disposed to the story, and that he sought the Senate's approval and confirmation to admit Jesus into the circle of Rome's officially recognized gods. The Senate rejected the Emperor's request.

Dreams his face is carved: According to Tacitus in the *Annals*, IV, xxxvii–xxxviii, Cassius Dio in *Roman History*, LVII, vii–ix, and Suetonius in his *Tiberius*, XXVI, Tiberius famously and repeatedly rejected divine honors for himself; he explicitly forbade that statues and busts of himself be set up without his permission, and when he did permit them, they were to be set up, in the words of Suetonius, "not among the statues of the gods, but as part of the decoration for the temples."

the face of Drusus: In A.D. 33, Tiberius ordered the deaths of Agrippina and her sons Nero and Drusus, all of whom he had earlier banished. The terrors of Drusus' death by starvation are recorded by Tacitus in *Annals*, VI.

Man is a madman clambering: Cassius Dio, in *Roman History*, LVI, xxix: "During a horse-race which took place at the festival of Augustalia, held in honor of Augustus' birthday, a madman seated himself in the chair dedicated to Julius Caesar and, taking his crown, put it on his own head."

These are my temples in your hearts . . . : This is an excerpt from a speech delivered by Tiberius to the Conscript Fathers in A.D. 25, rejecting a request from Farther Spain to erect a shrine to Tiberius and his mother, Livia, as quoted by Tacitus in

IV, translated by Naphtali Lewis and Meyer Reinhold in *Roman Civilization, Sourcebook II: The Empire* (New York: Columbia University Press, 1955).

The statue of a god: In *Tiberius*, LXXIV, Suetonius records that Tiberius dreamed of a statue of Apollo on his last birthday.

It is not the Roman custom . . . : Acts of the Apostles 25:16.

THE RESURRECTION

Vasari records the story that Piero della Francesca was blind from the age of sixty until his death, according to Vasari, at the age of eighty-six. He also reports that Piero's houses and property were burned and destroyed in the civil strife of 1536, decades after Piero's death.

When you were young, you girded yourself . . . : These are among the last words of the resurrected Jesus in the Gospel of John, 21:18.

THE DREAM OF CONSTANTINE

you saw rivers washing . . . : Taken from the *Latin Panegyrics*, V, an anonymous fourth-century oration to the Emperor Constantine, translated by Naphtali Lewis and Meyer Reinhold in *Roman Civilization, Sourcebook II: The Empire.*

the nails that fastened His hands: According to the fifth-century Greek historian Socrates Scholasticus in *The Ecclesiastical History*, translated and with notes from Valesius (London: George Bell and Sons, 1874): "Moreover Constantine caused the nails with which Christ's hands were fastened to the Cross (for his mother having found these also in the sepulchre had sent them) to be converted into bridle-bits and a helmet, which he used in his military expeditions."

The secret of the Empire . . . : Tacitus in *Histories*, I, iv, referring to the death of the Emperor Nero.

a stone that cries out in a wall: Habakkuk 2:11: "For a stone shall cry out from the wall."

We wish this church . . . : From a summarized text of a letter from the Emperor Constantine to Macarius, Bishop of Jerusalem, about the construction of the Church of the Holy Sepulchre, in the year 326, here translated by Cyril Mango in *Byzantine Architecture* (New York: Rizzoli, 1985), p. 15.

Though your men boil grass: That men out of hunger were driven to boiling straw and drinking the water from it is a legend of the Rabbi Johanan about the siege of Jerusalem, recounted by Chaim Raphael in *The Walls of Jerusalem* (New York: Knopf, 1968), p. 25.

Part Three / A Monument in Utopia

The epigraph from the Talmud is translated by Olga Marx in Martin Buber, *Tales of the Hasidim: Early Masters* (New York: Schocken Books, 1947). In another translation, in a discussion between Gamaliel and the Sadducees on the resurrection of the dead, Rabbi Johanan is quoted as saying in the name of Rabbi Simeon ben Jehozedek: "When a rule of Law (Halakah) is cited in this world in the name of a dead teacher, his lips move gently in the tomb" (Cant. 7, 10), translated by George Foot Moore, *Judaism in the First Centuries of the Christian Era: The Age of the Tannaim*, Vol. II (Cambridge: Harvard University Press, 1927), p. 382.

Throughout the poem, references are adapted from phrases and quotations from *Osip Mandelstam: Selected Poems*, translated by Clarence Brown and W. S. Merwin (New York: Atheneum, 1983), especially numbers 235, 267, 272, 306, 307, 329, 341, and 367.

Numerous details and references are adapted from *Hope Against Hope: A Memoir*, by Nadezhda Mandelstam (New York: Atheneum, 1970), including the following: that the first searches of Mandelstam's rooms were carried out by incompetent police interrogators, and that the Mandelstams' papers were stuffed into the most obvious hiding places; that Mandelstam read Alexander Herzen as a schoolboy; that often, even before his final arrest, Mandelstam was not in possession of a proper winter coat; that Mandelstam may have worn a yellow leather coat, which he traded for a half kilo of sugar, in the labor camp; that the word "money," written on a scrap of brown paper in the labor camp in a note asking that warm clothes and money be sent to him, is among the last words Mandelstam wrote; that Mandelstam composed not by writing with a pen or pencil but by whispering the words to himself—moving his lips—and then dictating the poems to Nadezhda Mandelstam.

1

glass panes of eternity: See the translation of poem #8 by R. H. Morrison in *Poems from Mandelstam* (Rutherford, N.J.: Fairleigh Dickinson University Press, 1990).

2

the frost's face: See the translation of poem #349 by James Greene in *Osip Mandelstam* (London: Granada Publishing, Paul Elek Ltd., 1980).

On the subject of Mandelstam's books and his bookcase, described
by Mandelstam in *The Noise of Time*, Nadezhda Mandelstam
writes: "In the hope of helping him to survive while his fate
was decided, I took a few books from our bookcase and sold
them in a secondhand bookstore, and spent the proceeds on
the first and only food package I was able to buy for him. It
was returned 'because of the death of the addressee' " (*Hope
Against Hope*, Chapter 51).

childless Petrograd: This is an adaptation of Mandelstam's "childless
Byzantium" in his essay *The Nature of the Word*, translated by
Jane Gray Harris and Constance Link, in *Mandelstam: The
Complete Critical Prose and Letters* (Ann Arbor: Ardis, 1979),
p. 120.

Like the Pharaoh's baker: See Genesis 40:16–22.

Who, then, that has lived . . . : This is an ironic paraphrase from
Michael Psellus's encomiastic description of the dying days of
Emperor Michael IV (1034–41), in Book IV of the *Chronographia*, translated by E.R.A. Sewter (New York: Penguin, 1966).

6

Novgorod is presented, in Mandelstam's poem #235, as an age-old
seat of resistance and rebellion against Moscow. In the chapter
"A Fur Coat Above One's Station" in *The Noise of Time*, Mandelstam describes the Novgorodians who "used to be depicted
as raging on their ikons," translated by Clarence Brown in *The
Prose of Osip Mandelstam* (Princeton: Princeton University Press,
1965).

That Stalin was the son of a "devout washerwoman" and a cobbler
who "savagely beat" him is from the article on Stalin by Ronald
Francis Hingley in the *Encyclopaedia Britannica*, 15th edition.

Doodling wolves in red ink: Reported to be the last observed activity
of Stalin, when he was last seen alive by a non-Party member,
in James H. Billington, *The Icon and the Axe* (New York: Knopf,
1966), p. 543.

7

They never asked themselves . . . . : From somewhere in Edward Gibbon,
The Decline and Fall of the Roman Empire.

each growing leaf from the old world: The metaphor of the repression
of leaves and the cutting away of branches from the old life is
Nadezhda Mandelstam's.

that mound of heads: According to Nadezhda Mandelstam, toward the
end of his life Mandelstam was tormented by a recurring fantasy
of "hillocks of human heads," as in poem #341. In *Hope Against
Hope* Mrs. Mandelstam quotes him as saying, with reference to
Stalin: "Whenever I think of *him*, I see heads, mounds of heads.
What is he doing with all those heads?"